Israel's Hidden Warriors

ESPIONAGE AND VALOR

CONTENTS

PREFACE

The book you are about to read is a glimpse into the extraordinary missions and operations undertaken by Israel's intelligence community; specifically Mossad. These stories, though fictionalized in certain respects, are inspired by real events and the tireless efforts of agents who work in the shadows, often unknown and uncelebrated.

This book paints a vivid picture of the high-stakes world of espionage and military operations, where decisions made in the dead of night can change the course of history. From the dusty streets of Alexandria in the 1950s to the covert cyber operations in Tehran in 2024, each chapter reveals a part of Israel's intelligence legacy, marked by ingenuity, courage, and the relentless pursuit of national security.

At the core of this story is Levi Asher, a fictional agent whose journey mirrors the real heroes of Mossad; those who risk their lives to protect their homeland. As you turn these pages, you will witness the careful planning, daring missions, and the intense personal sacrifices made in the service of a nation constantly under threat. This book is a tribute to the bravery of these individuals and the unwavering strength of the Israeli forces in the face of adversity.

While the events and characters are dramatized, the spirit of this work is very real. Israel's history is filled with moments where intelligence efforts have made the difference between survival and destruction. This book takes you on a journey through some of the most critical and daring operations that shaped Israel's past, present, and future.

Whether you are familiar with the intricate workings of military strategy or a newcomer to this fascinating world, this book will offer you a thrilling exploration of Israel's intelligence victories, rooted in real missions, and the ongoing struggle to protect its people.

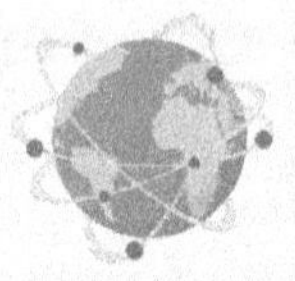

ISREAL ENDURANCE

Since its establishment in 1948, Israel has faced a continuous series of threats from its neighbouring countries and non-state actors in the Middle East. Born out of the ashes of World War II and the Holocaust, the Jewish people sought refuge in their ancestral homeland. However, the creation of the state of Israel was met with immediate hostility from surrounding Arab nations. This resulted in the 1948 Arab-Israeli War, where Egypt, Jordan, Syria, Iraq, and Lebanon launched an attack to prevent the formation of the new state.

Over the following decades, Israel's existence continued to be challenged by both neighbouring states and various terrorist organizations. The rise of nationalist and religious movements in the Arab world, particularly among Palestinian groups, created a complex web of threats, including the emergence of groups like Hezbollah and Hamas. These organizations, driven by both political and religious motives, have sought to undermine Israel's security through terrorism, rocket attacks, and suicide bombings.

The creation of Mossad, Israel's intelligence agency, in 1949 was a direct response to these ongoing threats. Mossad was tasked with gathering intelligence, conducting covert operations, and preventing future attacks on Israeli soil. Its role expanded over the years to include not only counterterrorism but also preemptive strikes, hostage rescues, and cyber warfare. With enemies on all sides—be it state actors like Syria and Iran or non-state actors like Hezbollah and Hamas—Israel had no choice but to develop one of the most sophisticated and effective intelligence communities in the world.

This book provides a window into that world; an exploration of how Israel's intelligence services have, time and again, been the difference between survival and devastation in an increasingly volatile region. From espionage in hostile territories to combating terrorism, Israel's struggle to secure peace amidst continual threats remains at the forefront of its national policy, and Mossad remains its sword and shield.

Eli Cohen (Mossad Agent)

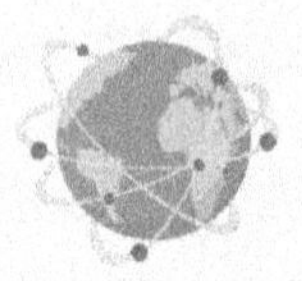

CHAPTER 1

THE BIRTH OF A SPY (1950S - 1965)
Alexandria's Son (1950s)

Alexandria, Egypt

Eli Cohen was born in 1924 in the vibrant city of Alexandria, Egypt. This city, with its ancient history and cosmopolitan lifestyle, was the perfect backdrop for the making of a future spy. Growing up, Eli Cohen was a sharp child, with a talent for languages. He could speak Arabic, French, Hebrew, and later mastered English. He wasn't just academically inclined, but he also had an incredible ability to blend in with people from different cultures, a skill that would serve him well later on.

Eli's family had deep ties to Jewish traditions, but the growing political instability in Egypt led them to leave for Israel in the early 1950s. His journey to Israel wasn't just one of physical relocation; it was also the beginning of his transformation into one of Mossad's greatest assets.

Mossad Recruitment

Once in Israel, Eli's unique set of skills caught the attention of Mossad, Israel's elite intelligence agency. In the 1950s, the Middle East was a volatile region, with rising tensions between Israel and its neighbouring countries. Mossad was always on the lookout for individuals with the right skills to infiltrate enemy nations, and Eli Cohen fit the bill perfectly. His fluency in Arabic and his deep understanding of Middle Eastern culture made him an ideal recruit.

The agency saw potential in Eli beyond his language skills. They recognized his charisma, his ability to think on his feet, and his willingness to make sacrifices for Israel's security. It was during this time that Eli went through rigorous training; learning how to operate as a spy, handle covert communications, gather intelligence, and most importantly, blend into enemy territory without arousing suspicion.

Espionage Training

Under the careful guidance of seasoned Mossad operatives, Eli was taught how to live a double life. He was assigned the alias **Kamel Amin Thaabet**, a wealthy Syrian businessman. His mission was clear: infiltrate the highest levels of Syrian military and political circles to gather crucial intelligence for Israel.

Eli's training was intense and exhaustive. He learned how to communicate in code, send encrypted messages back to Israel, and create believable backstories that would make his new identity as Kamel Thaabet unquestionable. Mossad trained him in how to navigate Syrian society, dress like a local, and even adopt their customs so that no one would ever suspect he wasn't one of them.

Relocating to Damascus

In the early 1960s, Cohen, under his new identity, moved to Damascus, Syria. This was one of the most dangerous missions Mossad had ever undertaken, but Cohen was calm and confident. His charisma allowed him to quickly rise through the ranks of Syrian society.

He was charming, well-dressed, and always seemed to have valuable connections.

Slowly, Eli began attending parties with high-ranking military officials, politicians, and businesspeople. His network of contacts grew rapidly. Everyone trusted Kamel Thaabet, the wealthy Syrian who seemed to have Syria's best interests at heart. But behind the scenes, Cohen was gathering and transmitting vital military intelligence back to Israel. From strategic military installations to defense plans, his information was crucial in giving Israel a clear advantage over its enemies.

Tension in the Region

The 1950s were a time of growing hostility between Israel and its Arab neighbours. The Arab-Israeli conflict was intensifying, and the Golan Heights became a strategic battleground. Syria was fortifying its positions, and Mossad needed someone inside the enemy's walls to get crucial information. Eli Cohen was that someone.

His network of contacts grew stronger, and the intelligence he was providing was invaluable. Mossad received precise details about Syria's military operations, including the positioning of artillery and defense plans in the Golan Heights. Cohen's reports played a critical role in shaping Israel's military strategy in the years to come.

Eli Cohen was more than just a spy; he was a man willing to sacrifice everything for his country. His ability to walk the fine line between friend and foe made him one of Mossad's greatest assets. But as his network in Syria expanded, so did the risks. For now, though, Kamel Thaabet was in control, and Syria had no idea that their most dangerous enemy was living among them.

Infiltration of Syria (1961-1965)

Damascus, Syria

By 1961, Eli Cohen, under his alias **Kamel Amin Thaabet**, had firmly embedded himself in the heart of Syrian society. His transformation was complete. He was no longer the humble son from Alexandria; he was now a wealthy Syrian businessman, well-known in political and military circles. Damascus, a city pulsating with political intrigue and military manoeuvring, had become his playground, and he navigated it with the precision of a skilled puppet master.

Building the Persona of Kamel Thaabet:

As "Kamel Thaabet," Cohen had an aura that made people gravitate toward him. His house in Damascus was a lavish mansion, often the setting for extravagant parties. The rich and powerful in Syria found his company irresistible; generals, politicians, and even foreign dignitaries mingled at his gatherings. These parties were not just social events; they were Cohen's perfect cover. Amidst laughter and wine, vital pieces of military information were casually discussed, and Cohen absorbed it all.

At every party, he made mental notes: troop movements, artillery placements, and most importantly, the Syrian strategies to fortify the **Golan**

Heights. His charm and insight into Syrian nationalism convinced many that he was a patriot, and the more he listened, the more information he transmitted back to Mossad. The stakes grew higher as his mission continued, but Cohen's intelligence was critical.

The Golan Heights

One of Cohen's most significant contributions was the intelligence he provided on the Golan Heights. The region was of immense strategic importance, situated on a high plateau overlooking northern Israel. Syria was turning the Golan Heights into a fortress, heavily armed with artillery and defense units. Cohen, under the guise of Kamel, visited military installations on the Heights, posing as a concerned Syrian businessman wanting to understand the country's defense efforts. Syrian officers, trusting him completely, provided detailed tours of the region.

Cohen's reports back to Israel were so precise that later, when the **Six-Day War** erupted in 1967, Israeli forces knew exactly where to strike. The maps and coordinates he sent helped Israeli artillery neutralize Syrian positions with devastating accuracy. His contributions saved countless lives on the Israeli side and led to one of Israel's most significant military victories.

A Rising Star in Syrian Society

Kamel Thaabet's rise in Damascus was meteoric. He had become a trusted confidant to many of Syria's most powerful figures. His influence even reached the highest echelons of government, where he could regularly engage with top Syrian military officials. The intelligence Cohen provided wasn't just about troop placements. He also sent Mossad detailed reports on Syria's political dynamics, its relationships with neighbouring Arab states, and internal power struggles. This information helped shape Israel's broader strategy in the region.

But with success came danger. Cohen's boldness in sending messages increased, and the sheer volume of intelligence flowing back to Israel began to raise suspicions. Some Syrian officers, though they considered Kamel a friend, couldn't help but notice how involved he seemed in military matters. Whispers started circulating about his true intentions.

The Fall Begins

By 1964, Eli Cohen's mission had reached its peak. Mossad had begun receiving longer and more detailed reports, but with every transmission, Cohen knew the walls were closing in. Syria, under increasing pressure from its military intelligence, started a counter-espionage campaign, sweeping Damascus for leaks.

In January 1965, Cohen transmitted one of his final messages from his hidden radio transmitter. Unbeknownst to him, Syrian intelligence had begun using Soviet-supplied radio triangulation technology, and it wasn't long before they located the source. On that fateful day, while Cohen was sending his most critical message yet, Syrian security forces stormed his home and arrested him.

Capture and Legacy

The arrest of Eli Cohen shocked both Israel and Syria. His trial, held in secret, revealed the depths of his infiltration. Syrian authorities were both furious and humiliated, knowing that their most sensitive military plans had been exposed to their greatest enemy. Cohen, however, remained defiant, maintaining his cover until the very end. Despite the best efforts of Israel and various international entities, Syrian leaders decided to make an example of Cohen.

In May 1965, Cohen was publicly hanged in Damascus. His execution was broadcast as a warning to Israel and the world, but instead of silencing his legacy, it immortalized him. Even in death, Cohen was a hero to Israel, his bravery and cunning forever enshrined in Mossad's history.

Cohen's intelligence had laid the groundwork for Israel's decisive victory in the **Six-Day War**. His reports on the Golan Heights and the inner workings of the Syrian military provided Israel with an unmatched strategic advantage. Though he did not live to see it, Cohen's legacy lived on, celebrated by Israelis as one of the most courageous and effective spies of the modern era.

Eli Cohen's infiltration of Syria was a masterclass in espionage. He lived among his enemies, charmed them, and ultimately helped Israel defend itself against overwhelming odds. His story, while tragic, is a reminder of the power of intelligence in modern warfare. His sacrifice was monumental, and his contributions, though cut short, shaped the course of history in the Middle East.

CHAPTER 2

THE SIX-DAY WAR (1967)

The Strike

Golan Heights, Syria; Tel Aviv, Israel

By 1967, tensions between Israel and its neighbouring Arab states had reached a boiling point. Syria, Egypt, and Jordan had fortified their borders, preparing for an all-out assault on Israel. However, unknown to Syria, Israel had a secret weapon; Eli Cohen's intelligence. His reports on Syrian military placements on the Golan Heights, gathered years earlier, had given the Israeli Defense Forces (IDF) the edge they needed.

In the early hours of June 5th, 1967, Israel launched a preemptive strike, starting what would be known as the **Six-Day War**. The success of this strike, particularly against Syria, would largely be attributed to Cohen's information. Armed with precise knowledge of Syrian defences, the Israeli Air Force (IAF) struck hard and fast.

Espionage

In the months leading up to the war, Mossad worked closely with IDF planners, sharing the intelligence Cohen had collected before his tragic capture in 1965. His maps of the **Golan Heights**, complete with artillery placements, bunker locations, and supply routes, became the backbone of Israel's strategy against Syria.

While the Egyptian front was a priority, the Israeli government understood that the Golan Heights was critical to the defense of the north. Mossad's analysis of Cohen's information gave the IDF a clear picture of the Syrian military's weaknesses. For Israel, the Golan Heights represented not only a military target but also a means of neutralizing the Syrian artillery that had been shelling Israeli villages for years.

Coordinating the Attack

In Tel Aviv, Mossad worked in coordination with the IAF to plan surgical airstrikes. Armed with Cohen's maps, they identified Syrian radar installations, communication towers, and key military bases. Using this intelligence, Mossad pinpointed the locations that would cripple Syria's ability to respond effectively to an Israeli offensive. These targets were relayed to IDF pilots, who prepared for the most crucial mission of their careers.

Combat

As dawn broke on June 5th, Israeli jets roared into Syrian airspace. The IAF's first targets were Syrian airfields, eliminating the possibility of an air counterattack. Then, with precision, the pilots turned their focus to the **Golan Heights**. Using Cohen's detailed intelligence, they bombed key artillery placements and defense bunkers. The Syrian forces, who believed they were well protected in their fortified positions, were caught off-guard.

From Tel Aviv, the IDF's high command watched as the operation unfolded. Within hours, Syrian communication lines were in disarray. The surprise and intensity of the attack left the Syrian army scrambling. Israeli ground forces, already stationed along the Syrian border, moved in swiftly to take advantage of the chaos. By the end of the day, Israeli tanks had breached the first lines of defense on the Golan Heights.

The success of the strike on the Golan Heights was beyond what even Israel had hoped for. Within two days, most of the Syrian defences on the Heights had collapsed, and Israeli forces continued their push, capturing the strategically crucial plateau. The fall of the Golan Heights not only secured Israel's northern border but also shifted the balance of power in the region.

In Tel Aviv, the Israeli government and Mossad reflected on the operation. The intelligence gathered by Cohen had been instrumental in achieving such a swift and decisive victory. While Cohen was no longer alive to witness the triumph, his legacy was felt in every strike and every step taken by the Israeli soldiers on the Golan Heights.

The Six-Day War was a moment of intense transformation for the region. Israel, outnumbered and surrounded, had managed to not only survive but thrive. Cohen's intelligence had been crucial in the Golan Heights operation, and though he had paid the ultimate price, his work lived on, forever entwined with the victories of Israel's military.

Consequences

Damascus, Syria; Cairo, Egypt; Washington, D.C.; Moscow, USSR

Conflict

The Six-Day War may have ended in Israel's favour, but the consequences rippled far beyond the battlefield. Syria and Egypt, humiliated by the rapid loss of their military positions, began to regroup and rethink their strategies. The capture of the **Golan Heights** had left Syria feeling exposed, and Egypt's devastating defeat in the Sinai Desert had shaken their military pride. Both nations were determined to strike back; but this time, they sought powerful allies.

In the weeks following the war, Israeli intelligence, spearheaded by Mossad, closely monitored the political developments unfolding in the region. Syria and Egypt had grown desperate. They understood that alone, they couldn't hope to match Israel's military might. So, they turned to the two global superpowers of the Cold War: The **Soviet Union** and The **United States**.

Syria and Egypt's New Alliances

In Damascus, the Syrian government quickly sought to rebuild its military. Israel's swift takeover of the Golan Heights had exposed the weaknesses in Syria's defences, and they knew they couldn't face Israel alone. Syrian leaders turned to the **Soviet Union**, requesting military aid, financial support, and advanced weaponry. Moscow, eager to maintain influence in the Middle East, responded favourably, sending a steady supply of tanks, fighter jets, and surface-to-air missiles to bolster Syria's depleted forces.

Meanwhile, in **Cairo**, Egypt's President **Gamal Abdel Nasser** faced similar pressure. The Israeli blitz had shattered Egypt's army in the Sinai, and Nasser was under intense political pressure to retaliate. Egypt, too, sought Soviet assistance, and the USSR was more than willing to provide aid, hoping to cement its strategic presence in the Middle East. Soviet advisors flooded into Egypt, training Egyptian soldiers and preparing them for future confrontations.

Mossad's Role

Mossad's network of spies across the Middle East quickly picked up on these shifts in the geopolitical landscape. Reports of Soviet military shipments to both **Damascus** and **Cairo** began pouring in. Mossad agents, some of whom had established deep cover identities within Syrian and Egyptian circles, relayed critical information back to Israel. It was clear that Syria and Egypt were preparing for another round of hostilities; one that would likely be even more devastating than the Six-Day War.

In **Washington, D.C.**, Israeli diplomats scrambled to maintain strong ties with the **United States**, knowing that their enemies were strengthening their connections with the USSR. The Cold War had created a dangerous proxy battleground in the Middle East, and Israel found itself in the middle of it.

The Americans, worried about Soviet expansion in the region, increased their support for Israel. **Weapons**, **intelligence**, and **financial aid** flowed into Israel, as the U.S. saw the small nation as a bulwark against communist influence.

The Brewing Storm

By 1968, the region was more volatile than ever. Syria and Egypt, bolstered by Soviet military hardware and advisors, were itching for revenge. The battle lines had shifted, but the animosities had only grown stronger. Israel, though victorious in the Six-Day War, knew that peace was fragile. Mossad kept a close eye on every move Syria and Egypt made, preparing for the possibility of a new conflict.

Damascus, once again fortified with Soviet tanks and missile systems, became a hub of Syrian military planning. Rumours spread of new alliances forming between Syria and other Arab nations, and Israeli intelligence worked tirelessly to track these developments.

While the Six-Day War had been a swift and decisive victory for Israel, its consequences planted the seeds for future conflicts that would continue to shape the region. The world watched closely as the Middle East entered a new phase of uncertainty, where Israel's survival depended not only on its military but on the careful orchestration of alliances and intelligence gathered by its most secretive organization, Mossad.

The Six-Day War had reshaped the Middle East, but it was far from over. While Israel enjoyed the spoils of its victory, the long-term consequences loomed large. The deepening ties between Syria, Egypt, and the Soviet Union were just the beginning of a new chapter in the region's history; one that would see Israel's enemies grow more determined and resourceful. Mossad, as always, would be at the heart of Israel's defense, standing ready for whatever came next.

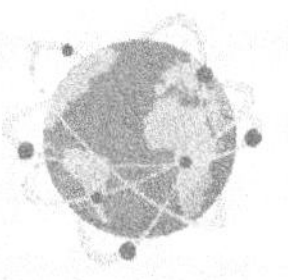

CHAPTER 3

SHADOWS OF TEHRAN (1968-1973)

Tehran Espionage

Tehran, Iran; Moscow, Russia

In the tense years following the Six-Day War, Israel's attention shifted to a growing threat from Iran. The world was changing, and Iran, under the Shah's rule, had become a key player in the Middle East. It wasn't just about oil anymore; it was about weapons. Israeli intelligence, always vigilant, picked up whispers of a dangerous collaboration brewing between Iran and the Soviet Union. The rumours? Iran was developing advanced ballistic missiles, and with Soviet support, these missiles could be equipped with warheads capable of reaching Israel.

The stakes couldn't be higher.

The Mossad, Israel's intelligence agency, immediately mobilized its top agents. A covert mission was planned to infiltrate Iran and gather critical intelligence. The goal: find out exactly what Iran and the Soviets were up to, and if the rumours of ballistic missiles were true, stop them before it was too late.

Espionage

Mossad agents were carefully selected for the Tehran mission. Among them was **Levi Asher**, one of Mossad's best cyber intelligence experts. Known for his calm under pressure and unmatched skills in hacking, Levi was tasked with leading the operation. His mission was simple yet incredibly dangerous: infiltrate Iran's defense systems and find any trace of ballistic missile development.

The first step was to establish a presence in Tehran. Mossad had already planted deep-cover agents in the city, posing as businessmen, diplomats, and academics. Levi and his team made contact with these agents upon arrival. They worked out of a nondescript apartment in northern Tehran, blending into the bustling metropolis, where few would suspect that Israel's top spies were operating under the radar.

Using state-of-the-art technology, the Mossad team began tracking suspicious activities in Iran's military facilities. They tapped phone lines, intercepted encrypted messages, and hacked into defense ministry databases. The most critical target was **Shahroud**, a highly secure military facility north of Tehran, rumoured to be the center of Iran's missile development.

Levi's team discovered encrypted communications between Iranian military officials and their Soviet counterparts, confirming their worst fears; missile shipments had begun arriving from Moscow. Iran's goal was clear: they were developing long-range ballistic missiles capable of carrying nuclear warheads. Mossad immediately relayed this information to Tel Aviv.

Conflict

As tensions escalated, Levi Asher found himself at the heart of one of Mossad's most daring operations. He had to hack into **Tehran's defense systems**, a nearly impossible feat given the layers of security. However, with the help of an Iranian scientist sympathetic to Israel's cause, Levi's team gained access to the Shahroud facility's inner workings.

In a darkened room in their Tehran safe house, Levi sat before his computer, typing furiously as streams of code flashed across the screen. He was hacking into Iran's top-secret defense servers, looking for any data on their missile program. Every keystroke had to be precise; one wrong move could trigger an alert and compromise the entire mission.

As Levi worked, tension mounted. They were operating on borrowed time. Outside, the Iranian Revolutionary Guard was conducting routine patrols. If any of them grew suspicious of the Mossad team, their cover could be blown.

After hours of painstaking effort, Levi finally broke through the firewall protecting Iran's missile development files. What he found confirmed their worst fears: the missiles were far more advanced than anticipated. The Soviets had provided Iran with cutting-edge guidance systems, and the missiles were already capable of reaching **Tel Aviv**. Worse yet, the final phase of development, which involved equipping the missiles with nuclear warheads, was scheduled to be completed within months.

Levi immediately transferred the data to Tel Aviv. The Mossad agents couldn't stay in Tehran much longer. The Iranians would eventually notice the breach in their systems, and when they did, they would hunt down whoever was responsible.

In the dead of night, Levi and his team dismantled their equipment, erasing all traces of their presence. They knew they had only days, maybe hours, before Tehran's security forces came knocking. Their mission was complete, but they still had to make it out of Iran alive.

The intelligence gathered by Mossad's Tehran team proved invaluable. Levi Asher and his agents had uncovered a plot that could have shifted the balance of power in the Middle East forever. Israel, now aware of

Iran's capabilities, had to act quickly. The next move would involve not just intelligence, but military action; a preemptive strike to neutralize the missile threat before it could be fully realized.

But for now, Levi and his team had to escape Tehran, a city that was growing more dangerous by the second. The shadows of espionage had darkened over Iran, and the game of survival was far from over.

The Yom Kippur War (1973)

Israel, Syria, Egypt.

Combat

On October 6, 1973, as Israel observed the holiest day in its calendar, Yom Kippur, the silence of prayer was shattered by the thunderous sound of artillery. In a coordinated attack, **Egypt** and **Syria** launched a surprise offensive against Israel, catching its defences off guard. The Yom Kippur War had begun.

The Israeli Defense Forces (IDF) were immediately thrust into action, fighting on two fronts: in the **Sinai**

Peninsula, where Egyptian forces crossed the Suez Canal, and in the **Golan Heights**, where Syrian troops pushed through Israel's defences.

Egypt and Syria's Offensive:

Egyptian forces, led by **President Anwar Sadat**, had planned their attack meticulously. They had assembled an overwhelming number of soldiers, tanks, and artillery, quickly overwhelming Israeli positions in the Sinai Peninsula. Egyptian soldiers used Soviet-supplied **SAM-6 missiles** to shoot down Israeli aircraft, a key part of their strategy to dominate the skies.

At the same time, **Syrian** forces, bolstered by Soviet weapons and advisors, launched a full-scale attack on the Golan Heights. Their goal was to recapture the strategic plateau lost to Israel during the Six-Day War. Syrian tanks rolled across the border in waves, forcing Israel's thinly spread forces to retreat.

For the first time in its history, Israel found itself on the defensive, struggling to repel enemy forces that had carefully timed their assault when Israel was most vulnerable.

Mossad's Role

While the initial shock of the attack left Israeli forces scrambling to regroup, Mossad's prior intelligence work proved critical to understanding the broader strategy behind the war. In the months leading up to the conflict, Mossad had intercepted communications between **Iran** and **Russia** that revealed significant military cooperation. The intel pointed to the fact that both Egypt and Syria had received massive shipments of Soviet-made weaponry, and that they were planning an attack against Israel.

Levi Asher's earlier mission in Tehran, where he had uncovered Iran's involvement in military dealings with the Soviet Union, had been vital. It helped the IDF piece together the movements of Soviet advisors and track the flow of weapons from Moscow to Cairo and Damascus. Israeli generals used this intelligence to predict enemy manoeuvres, giving Israel a slight edge despite being caught off guard.

This intelligence, though incomplete, enabled Israel to adapt quickly to the Syrian and Egyptian offensives. With real-time updates from Mossad agents embedded within enemy territories, Israel was able to launch rapid counterattacks on both fronts.

The Battle for the Golan Heights

The Golan Heights saw some of the fiercest fighting of the war. Syrian forces, armed with **T-62 tanks** and thousands of troops, advanced deep into Israeli-held territory. Israeli forces, vastly outnumbered, held their ground in a desperate struggle to prevent the fall of the plateau. Every hill, every trench became a battleground.

In one of the most critical moments of the war, **Zvika Greengold**, an Israeli tank commander, led a handful of tanks against a full Syrian armoured division. He and his men managed to hold off the Syrian advance, buying Israel the precious time it needed to mobilize its reserves.

Thanks to Mossad's foresight, the IDF had also prepared countermeasures to Syrian strategies. Israeli jets, guided by intelligence about Syrian anti-aircraft positions, struck key targets behind enemy lines. Syrian supply lines were bombed, and their momentum slowed.

Egyptian Front: The Sinai Peninsula:

On the southern front, the **Egyptian** forces had crossed the Suez Canal and established strong positions in the Sinai Peninsula. Israel's initial attempts to dislodge them were met with fierce resistance. Egyptian soldiers used Soviet-supplied **RPGs** and **AT-3 Sagger anti-tank missiles**, inflicting heavy losses on Israeli armoured units.

However, as Israel's forces regrouped, the tide of the war began to turn. Israeli infantry and tank units, supported by **F-4 Phantom jets**, launched a daring counteroffensive. The IDF encircled Egypt's Third Army and cut off its supply routes, turning the battle in their favour.

The war, which lasted until October 25, ended in a fragile ceasefire brokered by the United Nations. While Egypt and Syria had made initial gains, Israel ultimately recaptured most of the territory it had lost. However, the war changed the dynamics of the Middle East. It was a sobering reminder to Israel that it was vulnerable, and the psychological impact of being caught off guard would shape its military strategies for years to come.

The intelligence gathered by Mossad, particularly from the Tehran mission, played a pivotal role in helping Israel survive this coordinated assault. It demonstrated once again that intelligence was often the most powerful weapon in a war, even more so than tanks or jets.

The Yom Kippur War exposed the fragile balance of power in the Middle East, and Israel realized it could no longer rely solely on military might to secure its future. Diplomacy, alliances, and above all, intelligence would be the key to its survival in the years to come.

Mossad's work wasn't done, and neither was the war. While the guns may have fallen silent, the espionage, the behind-the-scenes deals, and the shadowy conflicts were only just beginning.

IDF (Operation Entebbe)

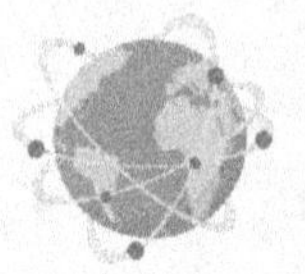

CHAPTER 4

OPERATION ENTEBBE (JULY 1976)
The Hostage Crisis

Entebbe, Uganda.

In the summer of 1976, an Air France plane carrying 248 passengers from Tel Aviv to Paris was hijacked by a group of Palestinian and German militants. The hijackers, armed and demanding the release of over 40 Palestinian prisoners held in Israel and other nations, diverted the plane to **Entebbe, Uganda**. They found an unlikely ally in **Idi Amin**, Uganda's president, who welcomed the militants and offered them support.

The hijackers separated the Jewish passengers from the others, holding them as hostages in the **Old Terminal** of Entebbe Airport. A 48-hour deadline was set: if their demands were not met, the hostages would be executed.

Back in **Israel**, panic and fear gripped the nation. The idea of negotiating with terrorists was strongly opposed, but every hour that passed brought the lives of the hostages closer to danger. Time was running out, and the government, under **Prime Minister Yitzhak Rabin**, was desperate for a solution.

Espionage

In the midst of this crisis, **Mossad** was tasked with gathering crucial intelligence that would inform the military's rescue efforts. Their first step was to locate and monitor the hostage situation, ensuring they had the exact layout of the airport and the number of militants guarding the hostages.

Mossad agents reached out to contacts within **Uganda's military** and government, some of whom were unhappy with Idi Amin's erratic leadership and secret dealings. Through bribery, manipulation, and covert alliances, Mossad was able to gain valuable insights into the positions of the terrorists and Ugandan soldiers stationed at the airport.

At the same time, Mossad relied on **satellite images** and **aerial reconnaissance**, which showed the geography of the airport and surrounding areas. However, it wasn't just modern technology that gave them an edge; Mossad had managed to obtain **blueprints of the Old Terminal**, the very building where the hostages were being held. These plans, combined with intelligence from insiders, allowed them to map out every entry point, every window, and every corridor.

High-Tech Surveillance and Real-Time Monitoring

The rescue mission would require precise timing and coordination, so Mossad turned to **advanced surveillance equipment**. They set up real-time communication channels to relay critical information to the **IDF** (Israel Defense Forces), monitoring both the hostages' condition and the movement of terrorists.

In a brilliant stroke of ingenuity, Mossad planted **bugs** in critical locations, including areas near Ugandan military compounds. These audio devices transmitted conversations between Ugandan officers and the hijackers. They revealed the terrorists' growing impatience and confirmed that the deadline for executing the hostages was real.

The Plan Takes Shape

Armed with this intelligence, Israel's top military leaders convened to plan a rescue operation unlike any other in history. Every detail, down to the minute, was scrutinized. The soldiers of **Sayeret Matkal**, Israel's elite special forces unit, were chosen to lead the raid. Their mission was as daring as it was dangerous: to fly into Uganda, land undetected, storm the terminal, and bring the hostages back home safely.

Mossad played a pivotal role in guiding the military planners. They provided precise intelligence about the number of hijackers, their weapons, and the position of Ugandan troops. Thanks to their surveillance, the Israeli commandos knew exactly where to strike and when.

The Stakes

Despite the overwhelming risks, the operation was approved. Every second counted. The terrorists were growing bolder, and the deadline was only hours away. The fate of over 100 Israeli and Jewish hostages hung in the balance.

The Raid

The plane was silent. Inside, tension thickened as Israeli commandos prepared for what was one of the boldest missions in military history. Through their earpieces, Mossad agents fed real-time intelligence about the layout of Entebbe Airport. Every corner, every guard, and every shadow had been mapped out through months of reconnaissance and surveillance.

"Remember, in and out in under an hour," whispered Colonel Yonatan Netanyahu, the raid's commanding officer. His voice carried both a warning and a promise of success. The team was focused, but there was no denying the immense pressure. Lives were on the line. If they failed, the hostages; over a hundred innocent civilians; would be slaughtered by the militants.

On the ground at Entebbe...

The Israeli Hercules C-130 landed, concealed in the dead of night. The team deployed swiftly, wearing Ugandan military uniforms to keep their cover intact for as long as possible. Mossad had calculated that they would have only minutes before the militants realized something was amiss.

"Move fast, don't engage unless necessary," Yonatan urged. They proceeded in the dim light, barely visible, navigating past the Ugandan soldiers that were patrolling the airport, who were clueless about the imminent assault.

Their destination: the old terminal building where the hostages were held. Mossad had sent agents to infiltrate Ugandan military ranks in the weeks leading up to the raid, learning crucial details about patrols, timings, and even the personalities of Ugandan officers who sympathized with the Palestinians.

"We've got them," one of the agents whispered into his comms, crouching behind a crate, binoculars trained on the terrorists inside. "Four hostiles confirmed. Hostages huddled in the far corner."

Inside the terminal...

The hostages, Israeli and non-Israeli, were huddled together. Some were crying softly, while others stared in stunned silence. A little girl clutched her mother's arm, her face pale with fear. The militants, relaxed in their positions, had no idea that the wrath of Israeli commandos was closing in on them with every heartbeat.

Then, all at once, chaos erupted.

The commandos stormed the terminal, gunfire rattling through the air. "Down! Everyone gets down!" Yonatan shouted in Hebrew as he led the charge. Hostages threw themselves to the floor as bullets zipped past them. In seconds, two of the militants were down, their rifles clattering to the floor. The others scrambled, but there was no escape. The Israelis were too well-prepared, too fast, and too precise.

One militant raised his weapon to fire, but Yonatan was quicker, sending a bullet through the man's chest. As the smoke cleared, the hostages were being led out, fear and confusion etched on their faces. "Move,

move!" a commando shouted, directing them toward the awaiting plane.

Suddenly, a Ugandan patrol vehicle approached. Mossad's real-time surveillance had failed to detect its movement, and now the commandos were exposed. Shots rang out again as Ugandan soldiers opened fire. Yonatan was hit, collapsing in the firefight. "Get them out of here," he gasped, gripping his side, blood seeping through his uniform.

The rest of the commandos returned fire, neutralizing the Ugandan threat. The mission was almost complete, but at a cost. Yonatan's body was carried aboard the plane as the remaining commandos and hostages made their escape.

Back at the base in Tel Aviv...

The news of the raid's success spread like wildfire. The hostages were safe, but the cost weighed heavy. Yonatan Netanyahu's sacrifice would forever be remembered as the price paid for freedom.

Prime Minister Yitzhak Rabin addressed the nation later that night, his voice steady but emotional. "This mission was a testament to the bravery and skill of our forces. Yonatan Netanyahu gave his life for his people, and today, we honour his sacrifice."

The operation was a success, a shining example of Mossad's precision and Israel's refusal to bow to terrorism. Operation Entebbe would go down in history as one of the most daring and successful rescue missions ever conducted.

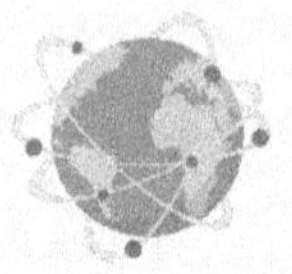

CHAPTER 5

INFILTRATING BEIRUT (1982)

Espionage in Lebanon

Beirut, 1982. The city was a powder keg of violence, caught in the crosshairs of regional conflicts, and it was about to become the stage for one of Mossad's most perilous missions.

Levi Asher, a veteran Mossad agent, found himself in the heart of Beirut, operating under the alias of Khaled, a Lebanese businessman with ties to the local arms trade. His mission was straightforward, yet incredibly dangerous: infiltrate Hezbollah's inner circle and gather intelligence on an imminent shipment of long-range missiles from Iran.

As Levi stood on the balcony of his rented apartment, overlooking the war-torn streets of Beirut, he couldn't shake the feeling that time was running out. Mossad had intercepted fragmented intelligence suggesting that Hezbollah had acquired advanced missile technology capable of reaching Israeli cities. But they needed confirmation. The mission was critical. If they couldn't gather solid intel on the shipment, Israel could be blindsided by a devastating attack.

At the Mossad Safehouse...

Levi met with his team in a rundown safehouse, hidden in a labyrinth of alleyways. "We have 48 hours," he said, his voice firm yet calm. "Hezbollah's leadership is moving fast, and so are we. We tap into their communications tonight. We need to know where those missiles are and when they're arriving."

Sasha, his tech expert, set up a network of covert listening devices and mini-cameras disguised as common street objects. "Once we have their comms, we'll know exactly who's pulling the strings. If we play this right, we'll also catch the location of the missile stockpile," Sasha explained as she adjusted the frequency on a small device.

Levi nodded. "It's time. Everyone knows their role. Let's make this clean."

The Espionage Begins...

By midnight, Sasha had tapped into Hezbollah's secure communications network using an encrypted feed from a cafe near one of their compounds. Levi listened intently as voices crackled through the radio.

"The missiles are arriving at the port tomorrow," a voice said in Arabic, the signal faint but clear enough. "The shipment will be secured before sunset. Ensure the guards are in place."

Levi exchanged glances with his team. This was it. The proof they needed. "Port of Beirut, tomorrow evening," he repeated. "We move before they do."

But Hezbollah's leadership was paranoid. They spoke in code, and despite Mossad's state-of-the-art decryption tools, it took hours to piece together the final details.

Just as they were about to leave the safehouse, Levi's phone buzzed. A single message appeared: *"Your cover is blown."*

His heart pounded. Mossad had a network of local informants, and one of them must have picked up chatter on the streets. "We need to move, now!" Levi barked. The safehouse was no longer secure, and Hezbollah's eyes were everywhere.

The Chase Through Beirut...

They sprinted into the chaotic streets of Beirut, where warlords, militia, and foreign agents blurred the lines between friend and foe. Levi weaved through the narrow streets, knowing full well that Hezbollah's forces weren't far behind. He could feel eyes on him from every alley, every window.

"Keep moving!" Sasha shouted, barely dodging a hail of gunfire that erupted from a nearby building. Hezbollah operatives, armed with AK-47s, were on their trail, firing indiscriminately as they gave chase.

Levi led his team through a maze of war-torn buildings, ducking into doorways and using the city's rubble as cover. "This way!" he yelled, pointing toward a narrow alley that led to the waterfront.

With Hezbollah closing in, Levi had one last option. "Sasha, get to the extraction point!" he commanded. "I'll draw them away."

"No way, Levi! We're in this together!" Sasha protested, but Levi didn't hesitate. He sprinted down a different alley, creating a diversion, allowing Sasha and the rest of the team to escape.

At the Port of Beirut...

Levi reached the port just as the sun began to rise. His diversion had worked, but he was running out of time. He crouched behind a stack of shipping containers, watching as Hezbollah's operatives secured the missile shipment.

"This is Levi," he whispered into his radio. "Target confirmed. They're loading the missiles onto trucks now. We need air support ASAP."

The signal was weak, but he knew Mossad had heard him. Within minutes, the sound of Israeli jets roared overhead. A strike was coming, and Levi needed to get clear before it hit.

Israeli Invasion

The sun rose over southern Lebanon on a clear June morning, but the atmosphere was thick with tension. Levi Asher, still reeling from the close call with Hezbollah, watched as Israeli military units mobilized for a full-scale invasion. Intelligence gathered from Mossad had pinpointed crucial Hezbollah strongholds, and today, the IDF was prepared to strike.

The Command Center...

In a makeshift command center just outside the border, Israeli officers gathered around a large map spread across a table. Levi stood among them, heart pounding. He had witnessed firsthand the dangerous weaponry Hezbollah was amassing, and now he had the chance to help neutralize that threat.

General Katz, a seasoned veteran, looked at Levi. "Your intel was vital in identifying their missile supply routes. We need to disrupt them before they launch."

Levi nodded, recalling the chatter he intercepted. "They've moved the missiles to a warehouse near Tyre. It's heavily guarded, but there's a vulnerability. I heard they plan to rotate the guards at midnight."

The general leaned closer, eyes narrowed. "Good work, Levi. We'll execute a precision strike tonight, but we need eyes on the ground. Can you lead a team in?"

With the stakes high, Levi accepted the responsibility. He felt a mix of fear and adrenaline; this was more than just a mission; it was a chance to protect his homeland.

The Invasion Begins...

As dusk fell, Levi and a small unit of elite commandos crept through the hills overlooking Tyre. They could see the warehouse lit up, a hive of activity as Hezbollah fighters moved supplies and equipment under the watchful eyes of armed guards.

"Stay low," Levi whispered, motioning for the team to follow him into a thicket of bushes. "We'll wait for the guard rotation to move in."

The plan was simple yet dangerous. They would use the element of surprise, relying on Mossad's intel to catch Hezbollah off guard. As they watched, the guards began to change shifts, moving away from their posts.

"Now!" Levi signalled, and they dashed toward the warehouse, weapons ready.

The Assault...

Once inside, chaos erupted. Levi and his team swiftly engaged the surprised Hezbollah fighters, using their training and Mossad's intel to navigate through the warehouse.

"Cover me!" Levi shouted as he moved toward a storage area filled with missiles. The room was dimly lit, shadows flickering as gunfire echoed around them. His heart raced, but he focused on the mission.

They fought their way to the back of the warehouse, where Levi found what he had feared: rows of long-range missiles, ready for deployment. "We need to destroy these!" he yelled, coordinating with his team to set explosives.

Outside, the sounds of battle intensified as Israeli jets roared overhead, dropping precision bombs on other Hezbollah strongholds. The coordinated assault was going according to plan, thanks to the intelligence that had pinpointed every target.

The Counterattack...

Just as they set the explosives, an unexpected wave of Hezbollah reinforcements arrived, catching the commandos off guard. "Fall back! We're outnumbered!" Levi shouted; his voice barely audible over the cacophony of gunfire.

They retreated deeper into the warehouse, using crates for cover. The tension was palpable as they fought off the approaching fighters. Levi's mind raced; they had to hold out until the explosives were set.

"Five minutes!" he yelled to his team. "We need to buy time!"

The commandos worked in perfect sync, one covering the other as they repelled the attackers. Just when it seemed they might be overwhelmed, the warehouse shook violently as an Israeli airstrike hit nearby, providing the distraction they needed.

"Now!" Levi shouted, triggering the explosives. The warehouse erupted in flames, a fireball consuming the missiles and everything around them.

What happened later...

As they escaped the burning warehouse, Levi couldn't help but feel a sense of triumph. The operation was a success, and they had disrupted Hezbollah's capabilities significantly.

Back at the command center, General Katz congratulated the team. "Thanks to your intelligence, we've dealt a heavy blow to Hezbollah. This will change the balance in the region."

Levi felt the weight of their victory but knew that the battle wasn't over. As he looked out over the Lebanese landscape, he understood that this was just one of many challenges ahead. The war was far from over, and the shadows of conflict loomed large on the horizon.

Photo by Esaias Baitel AFP/Getty Images

CHAPTER 6

THE INTIFADA AND COUNTER-OPERATIONS (1987-1993)

Uprising

West Bank, Gaza Strip.

The year was 1987, and tensions were simmering in the Palestinian territories. As the sun set over the bustling streets of Gaza, the atmosphere was thick with a mix of hope and desperation. The First Intifada had begun, marking a significant uprising against Israeli rule. Young Palestinians, fuelled by a sense of injustice and yearning for freedom, took to the streets, throwing stones and chanting slogans that echoed through the narrow alleys.

In Tel Aviv, the atmosphere was equally charged, but with a different kind of urgency. Inside a secure Mossad headquarters, Levi Asher, a seasoned operative, studied reports detailing the escalating violence. "We can't afford to underestimate this," he remarked, glancing up from his desk where maps of the West Bank and Gaza were spread out like a battlefield strategy. "If we don't act now, we risk losing control over the situation."

His boss, a stern but insightful woman named Naomi, leaned back in her chair, arms crossed. "Our informants within Hamas are crucial. We need to identify the key players orchestrating this uprising. If we can dismantle their leadership, we can undermine the entire movement."

Levi nodded, recalling his earlier encounters with the Hamas operatives. "I've already made contact with a few informants who are willing to cooperate. They're scared of what will happen if this escalates."

"Good," Naomi replied, her voice sharp and commanding. "We need actionable intelligence; specifically, planned attacks. I want you to get inside their circle, Levi. We need to know what they're planning."

As Levi prepared for his mission, he knew he would have to blend in seamlessly with the local population. He donned the traditional attire of a Palestinian man; a keffiyeh draped over his shoulders, jeans, and a simple shirt. He practiced the accent in front of a mirror, wanting to sound as authentic as possible. "I have to be one of them," he murmured to himself.

The next day, Levi travelled to a small town in the West Bank. The streets were alive with the sound of children playing, women bargaining at market stalls, and men discussing the day's events over steaming cups of coffee. It was a world teeming with life yet overshadowed by a growing sense of unrest.

"Who's leading the protests?" Levi asked a local shopkeeper as he casually browsed through fruits and vegetables.

The shopkeeper, a wiry man with deep-set eyes, looked around cautiously before leaning in closer. "It's the youth, all of them. They are tired of living under occupation. But there are some powerful leaders within Hamas, too; men who know how to ignite a spark."

Levi listened intently, carefully absorbing the information. He knew that understanding the local dynamics was essential for gathering useful intelligence. "Do you think they will escalate their actions?" he probed.

"Of course," the shopkeeper replied, his voice low. "They're planning something big, I can feel it."

That night, under the cover of darkness, Levi met with one of his informants, a young man named Omar, in a secluded alleyway. "You have to be careful," Omar warned, his voice shaky. "If they find out I'm talking to you, it's over for me."

"I understand," Levi assured him, pulling out a small notepad. "But I need to know what's happening. What are Hamas's plans?"

Omar took a deep breath, glancing nervously around. "They're organizing a series of protests, but I've heard whispers of something more dangerous. Suicide bombings…against military targets and settlements."

Levi's heart raced. This was the kind of intelligence that could save lives. "We need to act fast," he urged. "Tell me everything you know."

Over the next few weeks, Levi maintained contact with Omar and other informants, gathering crucial intelligence on Hamas's operations. With each passing day, the tension in the territories grew, and so did the sense of urgency within Mossad.

In the heart of Tel Aviv, Naomi reviewed the intelligence Levi had collected. "This is solid," she said, nodding approvingly as she scanned the reports. "We can't allow these attacks to happen. We need to launch a counteroperation."

"Agreed," Levi replied. "We need to dismantle their leadership before it's too late."

As they strategized, the situation on the ground escalated. The protests turned violent, and clashes between Israeli forces and Palestinian demonstrators became a daily occurrence. Every stone thrown represented a deeper yearning for freedom, but also a growing rift between two peoples.

That evening, Levi received a call from Omar. "They're planning something for the weekend," he said, breathless and panicked. "It's going to be big."

"Where?" Levi asked, heart pounding.

"Near the settlement. They want to make a statement."

"Stay safe, Omar," Levi replied, already making plans to report the information to Naomi. "We have to stop this."

As the First Intifada unfolded, the stakes continued to rise. Levi and his team at Mossad were determined to protect Israeli citizens while navigating the treacherous waters of espionage and conflict. The shadows grew darker, and the fight for peace was about to intensify.

Counterstrikes

As the First Intifada intensified, Levi Asher and his Mossad team found themselves racing against time. The intelligence gathered from their informants indicated that Hamas was planning coordinated attacks across multiple locations in the West Bank. These weren't just isolated incidents; they were aiming for a wave of violence that could galvanize more supporters to their cause.

Back in Tel Aviv, Naomi and her team reviewed the operational plans for their counterstrikes. "We have to hit them before they hit us," Naomi said decisively, her voice steady despite the weight of the decision they were about to make. "Our goal is to pre-emptively dismantle their operational capability."

Levi leaned forward; his brow furrowed with concentration. "We need to identify their key leaders; those who are orchestrating the attacks. If we can take them out, we can disrupt the entire movement."

The team worked late into the night, pouring over maps and surveillance footage, plotting the locations of Hamas leaders in the West Bank. They identified a series of safe houses believed to be operational hubs for Hamas militants. Each location was marked with a bright red circle, a stark reminder of the urgency of their mission.

On the ground, tensions simmered. As Levi moved through the bustling streets of Ramallah, he could feel the weight of the unrest. Groups of young men gathered on street corners, exchanging whispers and casting wary glances at the passing Israeli patrols. Every moment felt fraught with potential violence, and Levi knew he had to tread carefully.

"Are you sure we can trust Omar?" one of his fellow agents asked during a briefing at a safe house.

"Trust is a luxury we can't afford right now," Levi replied. "But we need the intel. He's been accurate so far, and we can't risk missing out on this operation."

The tension in the room was palpable as they prepared for their counterstrikes. "We'll execute these operations simultaneously at dawn," Naomi instructed. "Precision is crucial. We don't want any collateral damage, especially given the sensitivity of the situation."

As dawn broke over the West Bank, Israeli forces moved swiftly and quietly. Armed with intelligence from Levi and his team, they approached the first target, a safe house in a densely populated area of Nablus. The team had mapped out escape routes and potential civilian areas to minimize risk.

"Remember," Levi instructed the team, "we're in and out. Quick and clean."

With the first target secured, they swiftly moved to the next location in Bethlehem, where another key Hamas leader was believed to be hiding. Levi coordinated the operation through a headset, directing the troops as they moved.

"Target in sight," one of the agents whispered. "On your mark."

"Go!" Levi commanded.

The silence of the early morning was shattered as the Israeli forces executed their plan with military precision. In a series of swift, calculated strikes, they neutralized key Hamas figures, sending shockwaves through the organization. Each success was met with a tense silence, a stark reminder of the stakes involved.

Later that day, as Levi reviewed the operation's success, he felt a mixture of relief and trepidation. "We've dealt them a significant blow," he remarked, staring at the reports coming in. "But we must remain vigilant. They will retaliate."

Naomi leaned back in her chair, her face a mask of concentration. "We've disrupted their leadership, but we must anticipate their next move. The Palestinians are resilient, and they will not back down easily."

Just as they finished debriefing, an urgent message came through. "There are reports of planned retaliatory strikes against Israeli settlements," an analyst announced, his face tense. "We need to act fast."

Levi's heart raced. "We can't let them succeed. We need to launch counteroperations immediately."

As night fell, Levi and his team began to prepare for a new set of counterstrikes. The streets of Gaza would soon be the backdrop for a high-stakes game of cat and mouse, where each decision could lead to either devastation or salvation. The stakes had never been higher, and the tension felt electric.

CHAPTER 7

OPERATION CAST LEAD (DEC. 2008 – JAN. 2009)

Hamas Espionage

Gaza Strip.

The air was thick with tension in the Gaza Strip as Mossad's intelligence indicated that Hamas had built an extensive underground tunnel network to smuggle weapons. Levi Asher, now an experienced field agent, was chosen to lead a crucial operation aimed at mapping and ultimately destroying these tunnels.

Espionage

Levi gathered a team of specialists who were well-versed in urban warfare and intelligence gathering. They utilized advanced satellite imagery to locate the tunnels, alongside informants who had risked their lives to provide critical information. One such informant, a local shopkeeper named Amir, had lived in the area for years. "You won't believe what's underground," he whispered, his eyes darting around nervously. "They are preparing for something big. I've seen the trucks."

With the intelligence from Amir and the satellite data, the team identified several key tunnel entrances. Levi's team set up a temporary base in a dilapidated building, using it as a forward operating center to coordinate their efforts. The atmosphere was grim, as they knew the risks involved. The tunnels were not just transport routes; they were booby-trapped, designed to catch any unwelcome visitors off guard.

Conflict

As the team prepared for the operation, Levi gathered his crew for a briefing. "We need to move quickly and silently," he instructed, pointing to a map spread across the table. "The tunnels are likely protected. Expect ambushes."

They set out under the cover of night, moving through the darkened streets of Gaza. The moonlight glinted off the crumbling buildings, casting eerie shadows that danced along the walls. As they approached the first suspected tunnel entrance, Levi signaled for silence. Each member of the team was tense, hearts pounding in their chests.

They reached the entrance, a seemingly innocuous hole covered by debris. Levi peered inside, the darkness swallowing the beam of his flashlight. "Stay close," he ordered, as they began their descent. The air grew stale and musty, and the walls seemed to close in around them.

Suddenly, a loud bang echoed through the tunnel, and the ground shook. "It's a trap!" Levi shouted as they ducked for cover, realizing they had triggered a hidden explosive. Dust filled the air, and alarms began to blare in the distance.

Levi's team scrambled back, their hearts racing. "We need to get out; now!" he yelled. They dashed back toward the entrance, but not before they heard voices approaching. Hamas fighters, alerted by the explosion, were closing in fast. "We have to split up!" Levi commanded, knowing they had no choice but to evade capture.

As they split into pairs, Levi and Amir took a side tunnel. "This way!" Amir urged, leading them deeper into the maze of passages. The walls were damp, and the sound of rushing water echoed in the distance. They found themselves in a chamber filled with crates marked with foreign labels. "Weapons," Levi murmured, eyes widening.

Just then, they heard voices again, louder this time. "They're here!" a Hamas member shouted, followed by the sound of footsteps racing towards them. Levi knew they had to act quickly. "We need to gather evidence and get out of here!" he said, snapping into action. They hurriedly took photographs and notes on the weapons before making a hasty retreat back to the surface.

As they emerged, the night air felt fresh compared to the stale tunnel. They rushed to a safe house where

Levi's team regrouped, breathless and adrenaline pumping. "We got the intel we need," Levi reported, determination in his voice. "Now we have to plan our next move."

In that moment, they knew the dangers were far from over. They had uncovered a vital piece of Hamas's infrastructure, but the risk of capture or worse loomed heavily over them as they prepared for the next phase of their operation.

Israeli Offensive

As the new year dawned in January 2009, tensions reached a boiling point. The Israeli Defense Forces (IDF), armed with the intelligence gathered by Mossad, launched Operation Cast Lead; a military campaign aimed at crippling Hamas's capabilities in Gaza.

The operation commenced with a series of aerial bombardments. The IDF targeted key Hamas facilities, guided by the detailed maps and intel from Levi's team. "We know where their command centres are. We know what they have," a high-ranking officer stated during a briefing. "We'll hit them hard and fast."

The sounds of fighter jets roared overhead as explosions lit up the night sky over Gaza. Levi, watching the operation unfold from a command center, felt a mix of pride and concern. "This is just the beginning," he murmured to his colleagues. "We need to ensure they can't regroup."

As ground troops advanced into Gaza, they faced fierce resistance. However, with Mossad's intel, they could predict Hamas's movements, striking with precision. Levi's heart raced as he monitored the live feed from the frontlines, seeing the IDF neutralizing key figures and dismantling Hamas's infrastructure. "We've hit their leadership hard," he reported, excitement in his voice. "This could turn the tide."

The offensive was brutal. Urban warfare erupted in the narrow streets of Gaza, and civilians were caught in the crossfire. Levi's team coordinated closely with ground forces, ensuring that each strike was calculated. "We must minimize civilian casualties," Levi insisted. "We can't afford to lose public support."

As the operation continued, Levi felt the weight of responsibility on his shoulders. Every decision, every piece of intel, could mean the difference between life and death for countless people. He knew that the challenges ahead would be immense, but he was committed to ensuring Israel's security.

As the dust settled and the initial phase of Operation Cast Lead came to an end, Levi looked at the screen displaying the aftermath. "This is just the beginning. We must keep pushing forward," he stated, determination etched on his face.

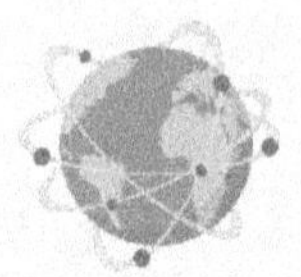

CHAPTER 8

THE HEZBOLLAH THREAT (2010S)
Espionage in Lebanon

The 2010s marked a new era of conflict and tension along the Israel-Lebanon border. Hezbollah, emboldened by its alliances with Iran and Syria, had been quietly amassing a formidable arsenal of advanced missiles. Mossad operatives, ever vigilant, detected a concerning pattern of activity in southern Lebanon. Levi Asher, now a respected figure in Israeli intelligence, was tasked with leading the mission to uncover Hezbollah's hidden missile stockpiles.

Levi gathered his team in a high-tech command center, the atmosphere electric with urgency. "Our intelligence suggests Hezbollah is not only stockpiling weapons but also preparing for a significant offensive against us," he explained, gesturing to a digital map showing various locations across Lebanon. "We need to confirm the existence of these missile sites and gather as much intel as possible before they can launch an attack."

To this end, Mossad employed a combination of cutting-edge drone technology and human informants. Levi coordinated closely with aerial surveillance teams, who launched drones equipped with high-resolution cameras. The drones soared above the rugged terrain of Lebanon, capturing images of the landscape that were carefully analysed for signs of military activity.

"We've got a visual on suspected bunkers just north of the border," one analyst reported, pointing to the monitor. "Look here; the heat signatures indicate something is being stored underground."

"Good," Levi replied, excitement brewing in his chest. "Now we need to infiltrate these areas on the ground. We can't rely solely on satellite imagery. We need eyes on the ground."

Espionage

Mossad agents began recruiting local informants, carefully selecting individuals who could blend into Hezbollah's environment. Levi met with one of the informants, a young man named Amir, in a dimly lit café in Beirut. "You must be careful, Amir," Levi warned, his voice low. "Hezbollah's watchful eyes are everywhere. We can't risk you getting caught."

"I understand, Levi," Amir replied, his voice trembling slightly. "But I have friends who can help. They work in construction and have seen the bunkers being built. I can find out more."

Days turned into weeks as the team gathered information. Amir's reports proved invaluable, revealing not just the locations of the missile sites but also details about Hezbollah's launch capabilities. "They're planning something big," Amir said one night, his expression grave. "I heard them talking about a potential strike on Israel. It's happening soon."

Levi's mind raced. The urgency of their mission heightened. "We have to act fast. If they launch these missiles, the consequences will be catastrophic," he declared, rallying his team. "We need to coordinate with the IDF to prepare a preemptive strike."

Conflict

As intelligence continued to roll in, the clock was ticking. Each day brought new developments, and the pressure mounted. "This isn't just about gathering intel anymore," Levi said, pacing the command center. "We're on the brink of an imminent threat. We need to stop them before it's too late."

With a sense of impending doom, the team worked tirelessly, piecing together the puzzle. Finally, they pinpointed the coordinates of a primary missile storage facility. "This is it," Levi announced, relief flooding through him. "We can't wait any longer. We need to take this information straight to the top."

Late one night, Levi presented his findings to high-ranking officials in the IDF. "If we don't strike now, we risk losing the element of surprise," he argued passionately. "Hezbollah is preparing for a significant attack, and we must be the first to act."

The tension in the room was palpable as the officials deliberated. Finally, one of them spoke. "We'll authorize a strike, but we need to ensure civilian safety. Precision is key."

Levi nodded, fully aware of the complexities involved. "We'll provide real-time intel to guide the operation. We have to do this right."

With the operation approved, Levi felt a mix of dread and determination. As preparations unfolded, he knew they were racing against time. "This isn't just about intelligence anymore; it's about protecting our people," he said, his voice firm. "We will not let Hezbollah succeed."

The Israeli Response

As the sun dipped below the horizon, casting a golden hue over the Israel-Lebanon border, the Israeli Air Force prepared for a mission that would send shockwaves through the region. Levi Asher and his team had done their part; gathering intelligence, pinpointing missile sites, and alerting the IDF to the imminent threat posed by Hezbollah's growing arsenal. Now, it was time for action.

In the command center, the air buzzed with tension. Levi stood alongside senior military officials, monitoring live feeds from drone surveillance. "The airstrikes will commence at 0200 hours," one of the generals announced, his voice steady. "We need to minimize collateral damage while maximizing impact."

Levi nodded. "We've identified the missile sites, but we also need to be aware of civilian structures nearby. Hezbollah often uses human shields. Precision is crucial."

Combat

At the designated hour, Israeli F-16 fighter jets roared into the sky, their engines cutting through the night air like thunder. The pilots were well-trained, aware of the stakes involved. As they soared towards the Lebanese border, Levi's heart raced. He monitored the operation from the command center, watching as the jets approached their targets.

"Target acquired," came the voice of the lead pilot over the radio. Levi could feel the tension mounting. "Engaging now."

A moment later, the sky erupted in flashes of light as missiles struck the hidden bunkers. The explosions lit up the darkness, a vivid reminder of the firepower at Israel's disposal. Levi's eyes widened as he watched the real-time footage on the screens. "Direct hits on all primary targets," he announced, relief washing over him. "We've neutralized a significant threat."

But the victory was bittersweet. As the dust settled, Levi knew that this strike was just one battle in a broader war. Hezbollah would not remain idle; they would retaliate. "We've sent a message tonight," he said, turning to the officials. "But we must be prepared for the fallout."

The days following the airstrikes were marked by heightened tensions along the border. Hezbollah leaders condemned the attacks, vowing to respond in kind. In their strongholds, they fortified their defences and prepared countermeasures. The response from Iran was swift, with officials calling for solidarity among their allies. "This aggression will not go unanswered," one Iranian general warned. "We stand with Hezbollah in the face of Israeli tyranny."

Back in Israel, Levi and his team worked around the clock, gathering intel on Hezbollah's reactions. "They're mobilizing forces," a junior analyst reported, eyes glued to the monitor. "We need to anticipate their next move."

A Cold War Begins

As the weeks turned into months, a tense cold war emerged between Israel and Hezbollah. Skirmishes along the border became more frequent, and both sides engaged in a dangerous game of cat and mouse. Levi knew that while they had successfully thwarted a major threat, the underlying tensions could erupt into open conflict at any moment.

In secret meetings with IDF leaders, Levi voiced his concerns. "Hezbollah is regrouping and strengthening its positions. We can't afford to lower our guard. They will seek revenge."

With every passing day, the prospect of renewed hostilities loomed larger. "We have to continue our surveillance operations," Levi insisted. "The last thing we need is to be caught off guard."

Meanwhile, Hezbollah sought to shift the narrative, portraying themselves as defenders against Israeli aggression. Their propaganda machine churned out videos of the destruction caused by the airstrikes, rallying support from sympathizers across the region. "This is not just a fight for Lebanon; it is a fight for all of us," a Hezbollah leader declared in a televised address. "We will not back down."

As tensions escalated, Levi understood the fragile nature of the situation. "It's a powder keg waiting to explode," he told his team. "We must remain vigilant and ready for whatever comes next."

The conflict was far from over, and the shadows of war loomed ever closer as both sides prepared for the battles that lay ahead.

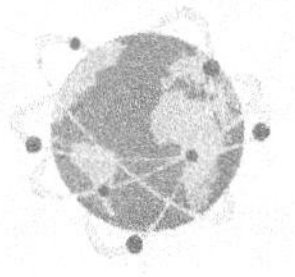

CHAPTER 9

THE HAMAS-ISRAEL WAR (2024)

Espionage in Gaza

Gaza, Israel.

In the heart of the conflict, tensions escalate as Hamas gears up for a large-scale assault. Their plans revolve around the deployment of advanced Iranian drones capable of striking deep into Israeli territory. With time running out, Levi Asher, now a seasoned operative, is tasked with a mission that could change the course of the war.

As the sun sets over Gaza, Levi studies the intelligence reports in a safe house, hidden from prying eyes. "If we don't act now, they could launch these drones before we even see them coming," he thinks, glancing at the map of Hamas's drone facilities spread across the table.

The stakes are higher than ever, and the pressure is palpable.

Espionage

Leveraging a network of deep-cover operatives embedded within Gaza, Mossad begins its work. Each operative has a specific role: gathering intel, tracking movements, and intercepting communications. They utilize state-of-the-art technology to monitor the drone facilities, feeding real-time data back to Levi's team.

"Operation Ghost Eye is a go," Levi whispers into his earpiece. "We need eyes on the ground. Remember, trust no one outside our circle." The air is thick with tension as the team splits into smaller units, their objectives clear: infiltrate, gather intel, and sabotage the drone operations.

In the dimly lit streets of Gaza, informants relay critical information about an imminent drone launch. One informant, a young local named Sami, nervously hands Levi a small USB drive. "This contains the launch schedules and locations," he says, glancing around to ensure no one is listening. "You must stop them before it's too late." Levi nods, knowing this could be the key to saving countless lives.

Conflict: The clock is ticking, and the mission becomes increasingly perilous. Levi's team encounters numerous obstacles, including Hamas checkpoints and surveillance cameras. "Stay low and move fast," Levi instructs his team as they navigate the maze of alleys.

As they get closer to their target, the tension escalates. They discover that the drone launch facility is heavily guarded. "We need a distraction," Levi suggests. A nearby construction site provides the perfect opportunity. With a few well-placed charges, they create an explosion that draws the guards away.

"Now's our chance!" Levi shouts, leading his team toward the facility. As they slip inside, the adrenaline rushes through them. Their goal is clear: disable the drones before they can be launched. Each second counts as they navigate the dimly lit corridors, the sound of their own heartbeats echoing in their ears.

But as they approach the main control room, alarms suddenly blare. "They've found us!" one team member yells. Panic sets in as they scramble to finish their mission while dodging enemy fire.

The stakes are higher than ever, and failure is not an option. Levi knows that the fate of many rests on their success or failure in this tense, dangerous moment.

Israeli Offensive

The sun hung low in the sky over Gaza, casting long shadows across the rubble-strewn streets. The tension was palpable as the Israeli Defense Forces (IDF) prepared for what would become one of the most significant military operations of the year. Armed with precise intelligence from Mossad, the Israeli command knew that this was a pivotal moment to neutralize the looming threat posed by Hamas's advanced drone program.

The Air Campaign Begins

As the first light of dawn broke, the Israeli Air Force (IAF) launched their operation, codenamed "Iron Shield." The roar of fighter jets filled the air as they soared over Gaza, armed with guided missiles and laser-targeting systems. Levi Asher, now deeply embedded in the operational command, monitored the situation from a mobile command center, his heart racing with both anticipation and dread.

"Targeting the first drone facility now," a voice crackled over the radio. Levi's eyes were glued to the monitors, showing real-time feeds from drones circling high above. The screens displayed detailed images of Hamas facilities, with several marked for destruction.

Strike Coordination

"Activate the targeting system!" Levi commanded, his voice steady despite the urgency. The room buzzed with activity as technicians worked diligently, coordinating the strikes with pinpoint accuracy.

"Facility 1 is a go!" came the response. With a swift motion, the operators pressed a button, and the screen flashed green. Moments later, a bomb was released from an IAF jet, hurtling toward the facility.

The Explosions

A distant boom echoed, and the ground shook. The bomb struck true, sending debris and flames soaring into the air. The facility, which had been key to Hamas's drone operations, was obliterated in an instant. Levi felt a rush of relief, but he knew the mission was far from over.

"Next target in ten seconds!" a voice called out. Levi's focus sharpened. He could not allow complacency to set in. Each facility held potential threats that could rain destruction down on Israeli cities.

Close Calls

As the operation continued, an unexpected turn of events unfolded. Hamas forces, alerted to the strikes, began launching counterattacks. Anti-aircraft missiles whizzed through the air, narrowly missing the IAF jets. "They've adapted quickly," Levi noted, his mind racing as he observed the chaos.

"We're taking fire!" a pilot exclaimed over the radio. Levi gripped the edge of his table. "Focus on the next targets! We have to keep the pressure on!"

Intense Combat

The IAF pilots, skilled and brave, maneuvered through the flak, executing tight turns and evasive actions. Levi coordinated with ground troops, relaying real-time intelligence to ensure that every movement was synchronized. Each airstrike was not just an attack; it was a chess game against a formidable adversary.

"Strike on facility 3 is clear!" The voice of a technician broke through the tension. Levi nodded, understanding the importance of this moment. He watched as the next missile struck, obliterating another drone storage site. The operation was a dance of strategy, skill, and the high stakes of modern warfare.

Victory and Reflection

As the last facility fell and smoke billowed into the sky, Levi felt a surge of triumph mixed with sorrow. They had struck a significant blow to Hamas's drone capabilities, but at what cost? Reports of civilian casualties began filtering in, a sombre reminder of the conflict's toll.

"Did we do enough?" Levi murmured to himself, reflecting on the nature of their work. "What's next?" The operation had been a success, but the questions loomed larger than ever.

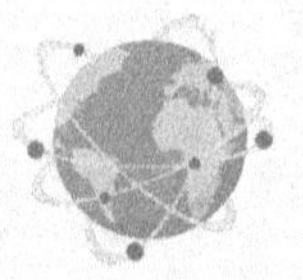

CHAPTER 10

THE IRAN SHOWDOWN (2024)

Espionage in Tehran

The year was 2024, and the tension in the Middle East had reached a boiling point. In the heart of Tehran, a chilling rumour began to circulate: Iran was on the verge of launching a missile attack on Israel using advanced Russian technology. The intelligence reached Mossad through multiple channels, and it sent shockwaves through Israeli defense circles. Levi Asher, now a seasoned veteran, was called upon for one last mission; a mission that would test every ounce of his skill and resolve.

Gathering Intel

Seated in a dimly lit war room in Tel Aviv, Levi reviewed the satellite images projected on the wall. "We need to confirm their missile locations," he stated firmly, his gaze steady. The images showed clusters of military installations in and around Tehran. Analysts buzzed around him, analysing data streams and intercepting communications.

"Here," an analyst pointed at a location on the map. "We've picked up chatter about a missile launch scheduled within days. They're planning something big."

Levi's heart raced. Time was not on their side. "We have to get inside their defense systems. We need someone on the ground," he said, determination etching lines on his face.

The Infiltration Plan

A plan was devised to infiltrate Tehran's military complex. Levi would lead a team of elite operatives equipped with the latest technology, including cyberwarfare specialists who could penetrate Iranian security systems. They would need to navigate the labyrinthine streets of Tehran and remain undetected by the ever-watchful Iranian intelligence.

"Under the cover of night, we will blend in with the locals," Levi instructed his team during the briefing. "We'll use the city's chaos to our advantage. Our target is the missile control center."

As they prepared for departure, Levi took a moment to reflect. He thought of the lives at stake and the weight of their mission. "We must succeed," he whispered to himself, knowing that failure could lead to catastrophic consequences.

Arriving in Tehran

Under the cover of darkness, Levi and his team arrived in Tehran. The city was alive with energy, a stark contrast to the tension that filled their hearts. They moved quickly, disguising themselves as local workers while keeping their eyes open for any sign of danger.

"We're getting close," whispered Sarah, a tech specialist with a sharp eye for detail. "The control center should be just a few blocks away." Levi nodded, his senses heightened as they navigated the bustling streets.

The Cyberwarfare Unit at Work

As they approached the missile control center, Levi positioned his team strategically. The building loomed ahead, guarded by armed soldiers and fortified by surveillance cameras. "We need a distraction," he whispered. Sarah pulled out a small device designed to disrupt electronic signals.

"On my mark," she said, fingers poised above the buttons. As the soldiers began to investigate a sudden power failure in the area, the team seized their chance.

"Go! Move now!" Levi commanded, and they slipped into the control center, moving swiftly and silently through the hallways.

Inside, Sarah and another operative, Amir, set up their equipment, ready to hack into the Iranian missile control systems. Levi kept watch, scanning for any signs of unexpected visitors. The tension was thick as they worked against the clock.

Countdown to Disaster

"We have about ten minutes before they realize we're here," Amir said, his fingers dancing over the keyboard. "If we can get into their mainframe, we can disable the missiles."

Levi felt his pulse quicken. "What's the status?" he asked, glancing back at the door. "We need to be out of here before they come looking for us."

"I'm in!" Amir exclaimed; eyes wide with adrenaline. "I see the control systems. Just a bit more…"

Suddenly, the door rattled, and Levi's heart dropped. "We've got company," he said urgently, moving to barricade the door. The sounds of approaching footsteps echoed ominously, and he could hear voices outside.

"We'll need to disable the launch sequence now!" Levi urged. "We can't let them launch!"

Disabling the Launch

"Working on it!" Amir replied, his voice strained. "I just need a few more seconds!" As the footsteps grew louder, Levi felt the weight of the world on his shoulders. If they failed now, it could mean war.

Finally, Amir shouted, "Done! The launch sequence is disabled!" Relief washed over Levi, but they had no time to celebrate. They needed to escape before they were caught.

The Great Escape

As they exited the control room, the atmosphere shifted. Soldiers flooded the hallways, alerted by the noise of their operation. "Run!" Levi shouted, leading the way back to the entrance. They sprinted through the building, adrenaline pumping through their veins.

"Cover me!" Levi yelled as he pulled out his weapon, creating a diversion. The gunfire rang out, echoing through the corridors as they made their escape into the night.

Outside, the city was still bustling, but Levi knew they had to blend in fast. "Over there!" he pointed to a side alley. They ducked into the shadows, hearts racing as they watched the soldiers flood out of the control center.

Mission Accomplished

After what felt like hours of running and hiding, they finally reached a safe house on the outskirts of Tehran. Levi leaned against the wall, panting. "We did it," he breathed, disbelief washing over him. They had successfully infiltrated one of the most guarded facilities in Iran and thwarted a potential missile attack on Israel.

"Let's get out of here," Levi said, determination returning to his voice. As they prepared to leave, he knew that this mission would haunt him for years to come, but it was a victory worth fighting for.

Israeli Assault

As dawn broke over Tehran, a tense silence filled the air, broken only by the distant sounds of engines roaring. Levi stood on the rooftop of the safe house, eyes scanning the horizon, heart racing with anticipation. He knew that today would be pivotal; not just for him but for the future of Israel.

The Call to Arms

Back in Tel Aviv, the Israeli government had been monitoring the situation closely. Prime Minister Sara Cohen convened an emergency meeting with military leaders and Mossad officials. "We must act decisively," she said, her voice firm. "If Iran is planning to strike, we cannot wait until it's too late."

General David Rosen nodded, looking at the maps spread out on the table. "The Air Force is ready. We can launch a series of airstrikes targeting their missile facilities and military bases. We need to cripple their capabilities now."

The decision was made: Operation Shadow Strike would commence. Levi, still embedded within Tehran, was the linchpin for this operation. He had successfully infiltrated the missile control center and disabled the launch sequence, but he needed to evade capture as the Israeli Air Force launched its offensive.

The Final Countdown

As Levi prepared to leave the safe house, he quickly gathered his gear; his heart pounding with the urgency of the moment. He was aware that the city was likely on high alert. "We have to move quickly," he whispered to his team, urgency in his tone. "Once they realize what happened, they'll be hunting for us."

He and his team slipped into the streets of Tehran, blending in with the morning crowd. But the tension was palpable; there were whispers of an imminent Israeli attack circulating among the locals. Levi kept his head low, navigating through the bustling marketplace, feeling the weight of the world on his shoulders.

The Sky Lights Up

Meanwhile, in the sky above Iran, Israeli fighter jets took off in precision formation, their engines roaring like a pack of wild beasts unleashed. The pilots were on high alert, fully aware of the mission's stakes. "We're clear for takeoff," Captain Eliana Levi, a skilled fighter pilot, announced. "Let's show them what we're made of."

As the jets soared over the Iranian landscape, their target was clear: military bases housing missile launchers and research facilities critical to Iran's military aspirations. Each pilot was acutely aware of their objective: to neutralize any threat that could endanger their homeland.

Striking with Precision

With impeccable timing, the pilots initiated the strikes, deploying precision-guided munitions on key targets. Explosions rocked the ground as missiles struck with pinpoint accuracy, sending debris flying and smoke billowing into the sky. Levi watched from a distance, a mixture of pride and anxiety swelling within him. He knew that every successful strike would bring them one step closer to ensuring Israel's safety.

Back in Tehran, alarms blared, and chaos erupted as military personnel scrambled to respond. "They're attacking!" shouted a guard in a nearby military installation. Levi seized the moment, aware that this was his chance to slip away unnoticed.

Evasion and Sabotage

"Now or never," he muttered, pushing forward as he navigated through the chaotic streets. The sounds of explosions echoed in the distance, providing both cover and a sense of urgency. He maneuvered past panicked civilians and military personnel, relying on his instincts and training.

Levi finally reached a secondary military facility housing the remaining missile stockpile. As he approached, he could see the tension among the guards rising, fueled by the ongoing air assault. "I have to do this," he whispered to himself, knowing the risks.

With determination, he set up his gear and prepared to plant explosives near the remaining missile silos. "This will disable their capabilities for good," he thought as he planted the charges with precision, ensuring they were set to detonate remotely.

The Great Escape

As he finished the task, he felt the ground shake beneath him from the ongoing aerial bombardment. "I need to get out of here," he urged, glancing at his watch. Time was slipping away. He activated the remote detonator and raced towards an exit, narrowly avoiding detection by the guards.

Just as he reached the outer perimeter, an explosion rocked the facility behind him, sending a plume of smoke and debris into the air. Levi could hear the alarms blaring and knew that every second counted. He sprinted toward a safe alleyway, determined to evade capture.

Back to Safety

Finally, after what felt like an eternity, Levi reached a rendezvous point where a vehicle awaited him. As he jumped into the backseat, he exhaled a breath of relief. "Get me out of here!" he ordered the driver, his heart still racing from the close call.

As they sped away from the chaos of Tehran, Levi reflected on the mission's success. They had not only neutralized a significant threat but also sent a clear message to Iran: Israel would not stand idly by in the face of aggression.

A Moment of Reflection

Back in Israel, the airwaves were filled with news of the successful operation. Prime Minister Cohen addressed the nation, praising the bravery of the IDF and Mossad operatives. "Today, we have secured our future and proven that we will do whatever it takes to protect our homeland."

Levi, safe but exhausted, felt a sense of accomplishment. The battle was far from over, but for now, they had triumphed. The operations of the past few decades had led to this moment; a moment that would shape the future of Israel for years to come.

"Good work, team," he said as they arrived back at the Mossad headquarters, a hint of pride in his voice. He knew that as long as there were threats, there would be those willing to stand against them.

CLOSING

A WORLD IN BALANCE

The Aftermath

As the sun set over Tel Aviv, casting a warm glow over the bustling city, Levi stood on the balcony of his apartment, gazing out at the horizon. The events of the past few years weighed heavily on his mind; a mix of triumph and loss. The air was thick with the scent of salt from the nearby Mediterranean, a reminder of both peace and the lingering threat that loomed over Israel and its neighbours.

The aftermath of the recent conflict with Iran had shifted the geopolitical landscape in the Middle East. Israel had struck hard, but the ripples of their actions were felt far and wide. Tensions with Iran and its proxies in Lebanon were palpable, and the spectre of another war loomed large. "We've bought ourselves some time," Levi thought, "but at what cost?"

The cost of war was not merely measured in numbers. Each mission, each life lost or saved, left an indelible mark on the fabric of society. Levi had witnessed firsthand the sacrifices made by his fellow operatives, the families torn apart by violence, and the civilians caught in the crossfire. He had devoted his life to protecting Israel, but now he found himself reflecting on the fragile nature of peace.

A New Age of Warfare

In this new age of warfare, the battlefield extended beyond traditional frontlines. Cyber warfare had become a key element of conflict, with Mossad leading the charge in counterintelligence operations. Levi understood that the threat of missile strikes, drone warfare, and cyberattacks would define the future of military engagement.

"We must adapt," he recalled his mentor, the late Eli Cohen, emphasizing the importance of evolving strategies in an ever-changing world. Levi felt the weight of responsibility to uphold this legacy, ensuring that Mossad remained at the forefront of intelligence and military strategy.

The Unfolding Threats

Despite their successes, Mossad's mission was far from over. New intelligence reports indicated that Hezbollah was stockpiling advanced weaponry along the Israeli-Lebanese border, potentially in preparation for future hostilities. The whispers of war echoed through the streets of Jerusalem, and the spectre of conflict lingered in the air.

As he paced the balcony, Levi's mind raced with plans and countermeasures. He knew that maintaining peace would require relentless vigilance. Mossad's operations continued, with agents deployed across the region to monitor and counter emerging threats. Informants were vital to their success, and Levi's team worked tirelessly to gather intelligence on Hezbollah and Iran's ambitions.

"Every moment counts," he muttered to himself, recalling his late-night briefings with fellow operatives. The balance between security and peace was delicate, and Levi felt the urgency to act.

A Fragile Peace

The fragile peace that had been secured came at a price. In the wake of conflict, it was easy to lose sight of humanity amidst the chaos. Levi remembered the faces of those he had encountered; the innocent civilians caught in the crossfire, the families of fallen soldiers, and the children who only knew war.

In the quiet moments, he felt the weight of these experiences. "Is this what we fought for?" he questioned. The relentless pursuit of security often overshadowed the human cost of conflict. Levi resolved to find a way to protect his country without sacrificing the very values he held dear.

A Hope for Tomorrow

As darkness fell over Tel Aviv, Levi took a deep breath, inhaling the cool night air. Despite the uncertainties ahead, he held onto a glimmer of hope. The Israeli spirit was resilient, forged in the fires of adversity. "We will face whatever comes next," he vowed, feeling a renewed sense of purpose.

In the distance, he could hear the faint sounds of laughter from a nearby café, where families gathered to share stories and dreams. This was the life he fought for; a life free from fear, where children could play without the shadows of war looming over them.

Levi understood that the road ahead would be fraught with challenges. Yet, with each mission, each piece of intelligence gathered, and each life touched, he remained committed to protecting the fragile balance of peace.

"Tomorrow is a new day," he whispered, turning back into the warmth of his home, determined to face whatever awaited him. The struggle for peace and security was an ongoing battle, but it was a battle worth fighting; for himself, for Israel, and for the generations to come.